BE MORE WONDER WOMAN

WRITTEN BY CHERYL RICKMAN

Wonder Woman created by William Moulton Marston

CONTENTS

FIND THE WARRIOR INSIDE YOU

Today it feels like we need Wonder Woman like never before. More than just a villain-catching, world-saving Super Hero, she is a noble warrior, one who protects the values humans hold dear: truth, justice, peace, and hope. Most of all, she represents the power of femininity – responding to aggression with compassion, speaking up with courage, and leading with emotional intelligence.

We all have a warrior inside us. If you want to know how to choose love over hate, courage over fear, and hope over despair, wonder no more. Wonder Woman will show you the way!

OTHER PEOPLE MATTER

The company you keep is important. Companions provide a sense of belonging, shape your beliefs, and have the power to lift you up – even when you're very different, like Wonder Woman and Etta Candy. So choose your companions wisely, and when you've found them, treasure them!

"No matter how small an act
of kindness or generosity or simple
positivity you put out into the world,
it will make a difference."

Wonder Woman

BE KIND

You may not be able to actually fly like Wonder Woman, but being kind can make your heart fly and your spirits soar. Kindness and positivity are contagious. They create a ripple effect that can inspire those around you. Helping others increases your own feelings of strength, makes you feel good, and reduces stress. What's more, the endorphins released provide a "giver's glow" and a sense of togetherness. So, give your imaginary tiara a bit of a shine, then carry out a few acts of kindness and bask in that wonderful glow. And remember: if someone is kind to you, pay it forward.

"We have a saying, my people.
Don't kill if you can wound, don't wound
if you can subdue, don't subdue if you
can pacify, and don't raise your hand
at all until you've first extended it."

Wonder Woman

TRY COMPASSION FIRST

Fighting should be a last resort. Even on the brink
of conflict, look for a way to defuse the situation and
deflect negativity. Trying compassion first will not
stop every battle before it starts, but it can help limit
the damage. Fighting gods and witches such as Ares
or Circe may have required Wonder Woman to use
force, but she was able to lead with compassion
when battling Strife and The Cheetah. Be like the
Ambassador of Peace. Make compassion
the first weapon in your armoury.

"When we fight for what's right,
we never fight alone."

Wonder Woman

WE'RE IN THIS TOGETHER

Wonder Woman believes people are better united
than divided. Together, we can work for a common
good. With a little goodwill, barriers often simply
melt away. So why not make a decision to encourage
rather than compete? Replace comparison with
compassion. Share ups, downs, and wisdom.
Get to know people from different backgrounds;
their worlds may not be as strange and faraway
as Wonder Woman's homeland, Themyscira, but they
could still open your eyes to new ways of thinking.

"If it means interfering in an ensconced, outdated system, to help just one woman, man, or child... I'm willing to accept the consequences."

Wonder Woman

PEOPLE MATTER

Connection is at the heart of what it means to be human. However right you think you are, it's never all about you. Everyone wants to feel seen, heard, and valued. So honour all voices by listening well; give people your full attention, maintain eye contact, ask questions, and show an interest. Then, like Wonder Woman, have the courage to speak for those voices that struggle to be heard. If a cause matters to you, commit to doing something – anything – to help.

"Those in need must always have access to alternatives; they must always have hope."
Wonder Woman

GIVE HOPE

Hope helps you cope. A positive outlook lets
you put problems into perspective and rise above
difficulties. Hope enables people to bounce back
after challenges, enhances problem-solving abilities,
and bolsters resilience. And, as Wonder Woman
knows only too well, hope can turn a battle around
at the eleventh hour, even when all seems lost.
So, wherever you go, be a beacon of hope to others.
Help them open their minds to new possibilities
and fresh ways of pushing past obstacles.
It's the greatest gift you can give.

BE YOUR OWN SUPER HERO

Wonder Woman doesn't wait for others to start the fight for what she believes in – she leads the charge. Be your own Super Hero. Look for ways you can make a difference, then go out into the world and put your magnificent Super Hero self to good use.

"All you have to do is have
confidence in your own strength."
Wonder Woman

BELIEVE IN YOURSELF

Consider what makes you uniquely you.
Is it your humour, curiosity, creativity, or courage?
Perhaps people admire your leadership, humility,
persistence, or integrity? We all have unique
superpowers. Making the most of your individual
character strengths can boost well-being and
performance and build a buffer against stress.
So forget your flaws and focus on your fortes!
Start looking for ways to use your strengths
in your daily life.

"People never know what they're capable of, Diana dear. Even a bird sometimes has to be shown it can fly!"

Queen Hippolyta

DON'T UNDERESTIMATE YOURSELF

As we grow older, we start to compare and despair and feel like we don't measure up to expectations. Try not to fall into that trap. Wonder Woman believes in our power to do good and keeps pushing us to do what we can to claim that power. Consider the tough times when you've overcome obstacles you never thought you could. Then hold your head high and step into your superpower! Your capabilities are much greater than you think.

"How we see ourselves
is who we become."

Wonder Woman

YOU ARE ENOUGH

All anyone can do is be the best version of themself. Even Wonder Woman! Don't let yourself be eaten up with envy or bitterness when you meet someone who is a little better than you at this or that. Instead, work on accepting that you are enough and appreciated exactly as you are, flaws and all. Of course, the desire to improve can be a great driver, but it's wise to balance your ambition for who you hope to become with appreciation for who you already are. Don't worry what people think of you – that's outside of your control, anyway. Just be your bold, beautiful, bodacious self!

"If this is a warning... I defy it!"
Wonder Woman

CULTIVATE COURAGE

Wonder Woman's abundant energy allows her
to act in bold ways. You can be emboldened too,
by taking a risk now and then. Decide whether you
stand to gain more than you lose – and if you do,
go for it! Daily life gives us plenty of opportunities
to be brave, even if for just a few seconds, whether
it's mustering the courage to ask someone on a date,
speaking up to your boss, or facing an old fear. So try
that bold hairstyle or audition for that talent show.
Quiet that nagging voice of doubt and
step out of your comfort zone.

"Be creative.
Be adventurous. Be original."
Wonder Woman

DANCE TO THE BEAT OF YOUR OWN DRUM

Do you sometimes struggle to fit in? If so, you aren't
the only one! It can be tempting to mask your true
self and follow others rather than go in your own
direction, but in the long run it's exhausting.
Instead, try going your own way and following
your own truth. Ignore any criticism from others;
eventually you will gain more respect. By celebrating
your individuality you can reduce the pressure of
social comparison and be free to get on with being
yourself. Wonder Woman has never been afraid
to dance to her own wonderful drumbeat.
What does yours sound like?

"Carry that courage and faith
just a little further now."
Wonder Woman

PERSIST

One of the greatest traits of Wonder Woman
as the world's preeminent female Super Hero
is her dauntless energy, grit, and determination
to do whatever it takes to succeed. Follow her lead;
keep going when you feel like quitting, focus on why
you want to achieve your goal, and avoid distractions
and comparisons. If the task seems too big, break
it down into mini-milestones and take small steps.
Remember, the only sure way of failing
is to stop trying!

HONOUR YOUR VALUES

Obstacles can seem less daunting when they stand between you and an ideal. That's because we're motivated by purpose. The values we hold dear and the changes we hope to make in the world get us fired up and give our lives meaning. So take up your metaphorical sword, find a cause, and fight for it!

"Oh, Gods of Olympus! Though I love Paradise, I yearn for more from my life. I yearn for purpose!"

Wonder Woman

FIND YOUR PURPOSE

What is your aim in life? What sparks your interest, stirs your dreams, and motivates you to take action? That's your purpose. A purpose is a strong guiding force that provides a sense of direction in life. Your purpose may not be saving the world, like Wonder Woman's (although it could be helping to save the rainforest). You might long to make a medical breakthrough, lead a political party, write a best-selling book, or just be the best you can be. Whatever it is, get up, get out, and go for it!

"What sort of world
do you want to live in?"
Wonder Woman

LEAD THE WAY

Wonder Woman wants to live in a peaceful world, where citizens of Earth are treated equally and with respect. What kind of world do you want to live in? What can you do to make it happen? Perhaps you want to live in a waste-free world or one where pollution is a thing of the past? These can seem like impossible goals, but know this: we are not powerless. So take responsibility, speak out, and above all practise what you preach.

"We have to live by
some sort of principle."
Wonder Woman

STICK TO YOUR PRINCIPLES

What values do you hold most dear? Kindness? Politeness? Integrity? Before you try to influence others, ask yourself whether the way you live your own life reflects these values. It's all too easy to come up with excuses, so ask yourself whether you're truly sticking to your principles. Be honest with yourself! Wonder Woman probably isn't around to give you a whirl with her Lasso of Truth, but a long, hard look in the mirror should suffice.

"League! All together!
We can do this!"
Wonder Woman

JOIN FORCES

Having a purpose is great. What's even
greater is finding others who share that purpose.
There's strength in numbers, and goals can usually
be achieved more quickly when there's a whole
posse pushing for them. So as you go about your
life, be on the lookout for like-minded people.
You don't have to form a formal team or organisation
like Wonder Woman and the Justice League.
Maybe you just want to meet up with them now
and then to chat or exchange contacts.
Who knows, maybe they will open your eyes
to different ways of going about things.

"I cannot preach hate and warfare when I am a disciple of peace and love!"
Wonder Woman

LOOK AFTER EACH OTHER

If you had a magic wand (or a Lasso of Truth), what would you change in society? Who would you wish to protect? And how far would you be prepared to go to achieve your goals? Purpose and passion are great, but beware of letting a too-fiery sense of justice lead to feelings of hatred for those who oppose you. That's a fast way of becoming the very thing you despise. Like Wonder Woman, fight the good fight to make the world a better place for everyone… together.